Table

Introduction

Comparer l'interprétation du jazz et celle de la musique 'classique', c'est un peu comme comparer la manière dont les Américains et les Anglais s'expriment. Les deux langues s'écrivent à peu près de la même façon, mais l'accent est complètement différent. La meilleure façon d'acquérir l'accent américain est de vivre dans le pays pendant un certain temps — on s'habitue à la sonorité de la langue, et on adopte naturellement le même dialecte. De même, avec le jazz, il est essentiel d'écouter attentivement les musiciens qui jouent dans le style, pour développer le sens du jazz dans son propre jeu.

Le but de ce livre est d'être utile aux musiciens qui ont reçu une formation 'classique' et qui veulent se mettre à interpréter le jazz à son niveau le plus élémentaire.

Comment utiliser ce livre

La première partie permet à l'étudiant d'assimiler les figures rythmiques essentielles de la musique de jazz. On commence avec la notion du rythme de swing, et on continue avec diverses façons d'anticiper sur les temps, et avec les syncopes.

La seconde partie contient vingt études de jazz mélodiques, classées par ordre de difficulté croissante. Elles utilisent les rythmes présentés dans la première partie dans diverses combinaisons. Des exercices de la première partie judicieusement choisis peuvent servir de matériel préparatoire aux études de la seconde partie.

La troisième partie introduit la notion d'improvisation en jazz. L'élève travaille les exercices de cette section tout en incorporant dans son jeu les idées rythmiques et mélodiques acquises dans la première et la seconde partie. Il reprendra ensuite les études de la seconde partie utilisera les chiffrages d'accords comme aide à d'autres improvisations.

James Rae

Inhalt

Einleitung

Die Interpretation von Jazz verhält sich zu der Interpretation von klassischer Musik ungefähr so wie die Aussprache des amerikanischen zu der des britischen Englisch. Die Rechtschreibung ist im wesentlichen die gleiche, der Tonfall aber völlig verschieden. Einen richtigen amerikanischen Akzent gewöhnt man sich am leichtesten an, wenn man einige Zeit im Land lebt und sich in den Sprachklang einhört, so daß es selbstverständlich wird, den Dialekt anzunehmen. Auch beim Jazz ist es wichtig, versierten Spielern aufmerksam zuzuhören, um ein 'Feeling' im eigenen Spiel zu entwickeln.

Dieses Buch ist für 'klassische' Musiker konzipiert, die sich die elementaren Grundlagen der Jazzmusik erarbeiten wollen.

Gebrauchsanweisung für das Buch

Im ersten Teil soll der Schüler die wesentlichen rhythmischen Grundlagen des Jazz kennenlernen. Den Anfang bilden das Prinzip des 'Swings' und die verschiedenen Arten von antizipiertem Beat und Synkopierung.

Der zweite Teil enthält zwanzig melodische Jazzstudien in fortschreitendem Schwierigkeitsgrad. Sie verwenden die Rhythmen des ersten Teils in unterschiedlichen Kombinationen. So können sorgfältig ausgewählte Übungen des ersten als Vorbereitung für den zweiten Teil dienen.

Teil 3 ist eine Einführung in die Jazz-Improvisation. Wenn der Schüler diesen Teil durcharbeitet, sollte er sowohl die rhythmischen als auch die melodischen Modelle der ersten beiden Teile verinnerlicht haben und versuchen, sie in seinem Spiel anzuwenden. Anschließend kann der Schüler zu den Studien des zweiten Teils zurückkehren und die Akkordbezifferungen als Grundlage für weitere Improvisationen nutzen.

James Rae

Progressive JAZZ Studies

Etudes progressives de jazz
Fortschreitende Jazz-Etüden

for B♭ clarinet – easy level

pour clarinette – niveau facile
für Klarinette in B – einfacher Schwierigkeitsgrad

James Rae

© 1993 by Faber Music Ltd
First published in 1993 by Faber Music Ltd
3 Queen Square London WC1N 3AU
Music and typesetting by Seton Music Graphics Ltd
Cover design by Shirley Tucker
Cover photographs by Ben Johnson
French translations by Frederik Martin
German translations by Eike Wernhard
Printed in England

ISBN 0-571-51359-X

To buy Faber Music publications or to find out about the full range of titles available
please contact your local music retailer or Faber Music sales enquiries:

Faber Music Limited, Burnt Mill, Elizabeth Way, Harlow, CM20 2HX England
Tel: +44 (0)1279 82 89 82   Fax: +44 (0)1279 82 89 83
Email: sales@fabermusic.com   www.fabermusic.com

FABER *ff* MUSIC

Contents

Introduction

Comparing the interpretation of jazz music to that of 'classical' can be likened to the comparison between spoken 'American' and spoken 'English'. They are both written in more or less the same way but sound totally different. The best way to acquire a strong American accent is to live there for a while — the sound of the language is absorbed and it becomes natural to adopt the same dialect. With jazz, it is also essential to listen carefully to players of the idiom in order to develop a 'feel' for jazz in your own playing.

This book is designed to assist 'classically' trained musicians with the interpretation of jazz music at the most elementary level.

Using the book

The aim in Part 1 is for the student to absorb the essential rhythmic devices of jazz music. It begins with the concept of swing rhythm, and then works through various types of anticipated beat and syncopation.

Part 2 contains twenty melodious jazz studies, arranged progressively. These incorporate, in various combinations, the rhythms established in Part 1. Carefully selected exercises from Part 1 may be used as preliminary material for the studies in Part 2.

Part 3 introduces the student to the concept of jazz improvisation. While working through the exercises in this section, the student should be encouraged to incorporate into his/her playing both rhythmic and melodic ideas absorbed in Parts 1 and 2. The student may then return to the studies in Part 2, using the chord symbols as a basis for further improvisation.

James Rae

1 ASPECTS OF JAZZ RHYTHM
Aspects rythmiques du jazz
Der Jazzrhythmus

Rhythm is arguably the most important element in jazz music, and a good sense of rhythm is one of the jazz musician's most valuable assets.

On peut dire que le rythme est l'élément le plus important de la musique de jazz, et un bon sens du rythme est l'une des qualités principales du musicien de jazz.

Der Rhythmus ist wohl das wichtigste Kennzeichen des Jazz, und ein gutes Rhythmusgefühl gehört mit zu dem wertvollsten Kapital eines Jazzmusikers.

Swing quavers ▪ *Faire swinguer les croches* ▪ Swingende Achtel

Lengthen the first and shorten the second of each pair of notes.
Dans chaque paire de notes, allongez la première et raccourcissez la seconde.
Die erste Note jeder Achtelgruppe wird verlängert, die zweite verkürzt.

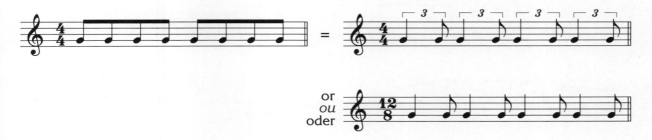

a) Try clapping the rhythm before playing
b) Always use soft-tonguing where no slurs or accents are marked

a) Essayez de frapper le rythme des mains avant de le jouer
b) Pas de coup de langue marqué sauf s'il y a une liaison ou un accent

a) Vor dem Spielen den Rhythmus klatschen
b) Immer mit weichem Zungenstoß spielen, wenn weder legato noch Akzente vorgeschrieben sind.

N.B.
All quavers in jazz (unless in a rock or latin context, or otherwise indicated) are played in swing time.

Dans le jazz, les croches se jouent toujours avec le rhythme du swing (sauf dans la musique de rock et latine, ou lorsque le contraire est indiqué)

Alle Achtel werden im Jazz swingend gespielt (außer beim Rock und bei Lateinamerikanischer Musik und wenn es anders vorgeschrieben ist).

Anticipation ▪ *Anticiper* ▪ Antizipation

Bringing forward the main beats in the bar by a quaver.
Jouer les temps forts de la mesure une croche en avance.
Die starken Taktschläge werden um ein Achtel vorweggenommen (antizipiert).

Anticipated 1st beat · *1er temps anticipé* · Die antizipierte Eins

9

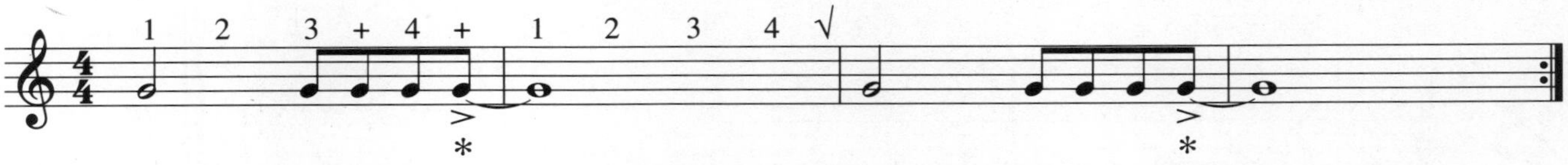

* It is stylistically correct to accent off-beats in jazz music.
Dans le jazz, il est correct d'accentuer les temps faibles.
Es ist im Jazz stilistisch richtig, die schwachen Zählzeiten zu betonen.

10

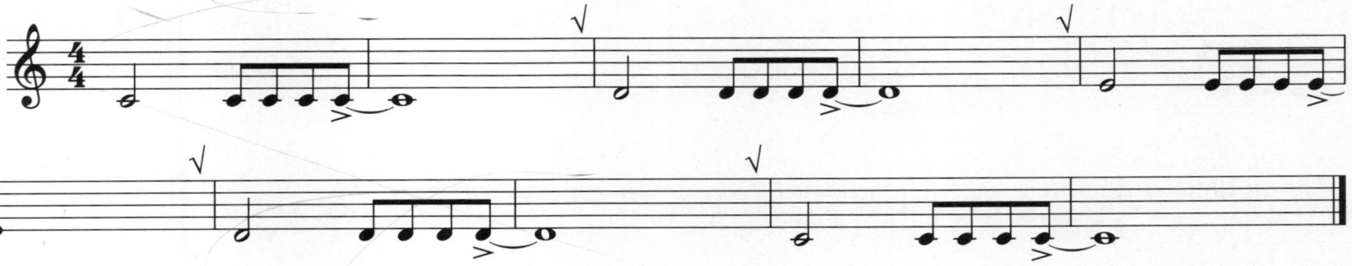

11

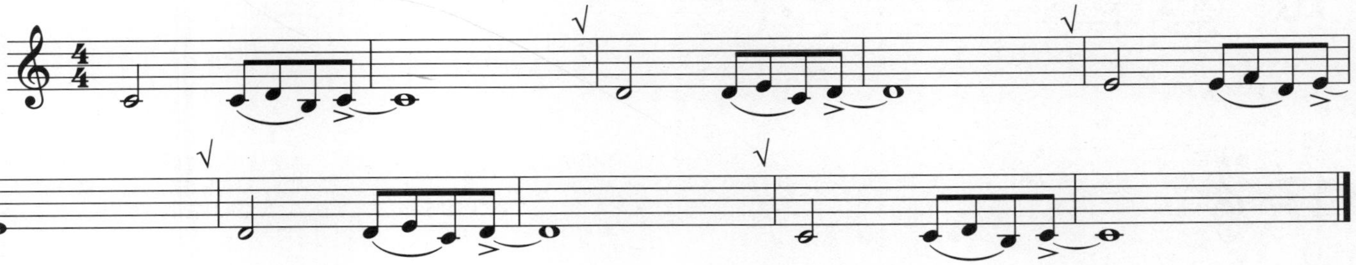

12

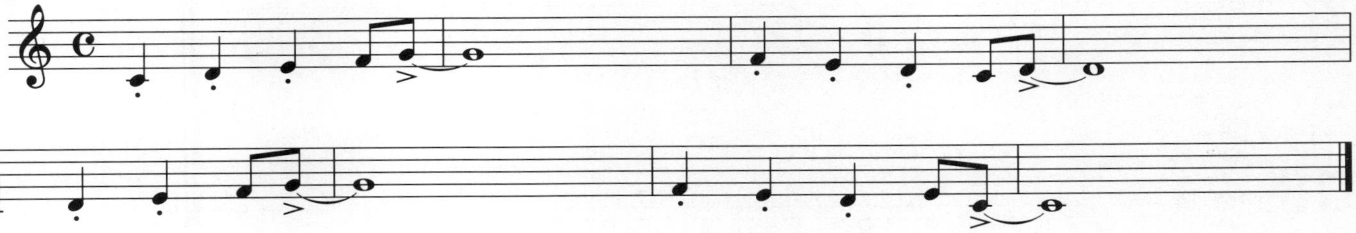

13

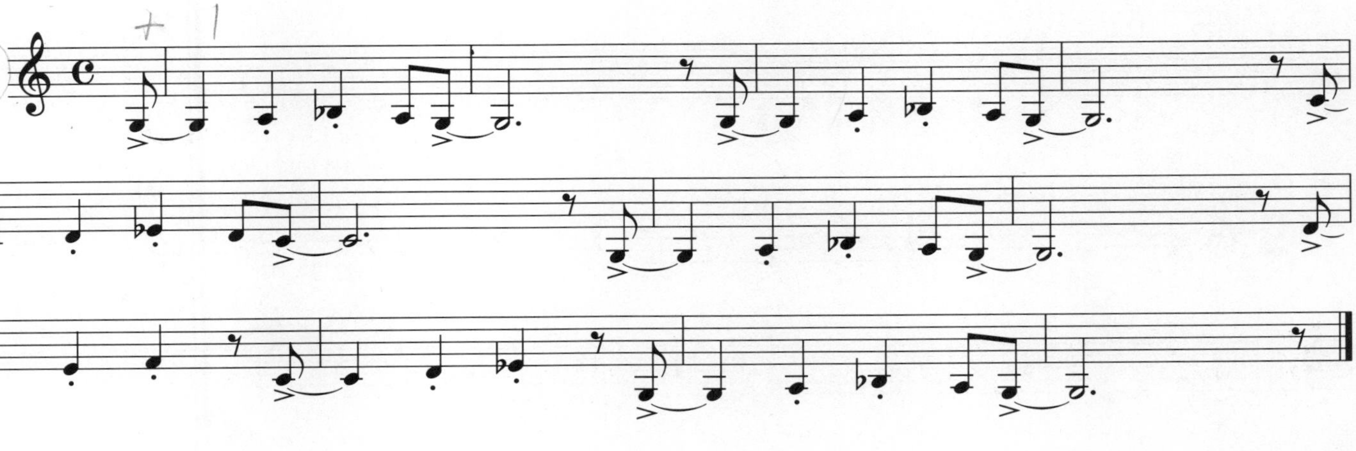

16/3/02

Anticipated 2nd beat · *2ème temps anticipé* · Die antizipierte Zwei

Anticipated 3rd beat · *3ème temps anticipé* · Die antizipierte Drei

6

Anticipated 4th beat · *4ème temps anticipé* · Die antizipierte Vier

_21/4/02_

F major seventh
G pentatonic } _SWUNG!_
A natural minor }

Syncopation · _Les syncopes_ · Synkopierung

Off-beat crotchets
Noires commençant sur le temps faible
Viertelnoten auf unbetonter Zählzeit

* Off-beat crotchets are generally played short in jazz music.
En général dans la musique de jazz on écourte les noires sur les temps faibles.
Es ist im Jazz üblich, die unbetonten Viertelnoten (off-beats) kurz zu spielen.

2 * MELODIC JAZZ STUDIES
Etudes mélodiques de jazz
Melodische Jazz-Etüden

* After working through Part 3 of the book, the chord symbols may be used as a guide to improvisation.

Après avoir bien travaillé la troisième partie de ce livre, les chiffrages d'accords peuvent servir de guides à l'improvisation.

Hat man sich durch den dritten Teil des Buches durchgearbeitet, können die Akkordsymbole als Leitfaden für Improvisationen benutzt werden.

10

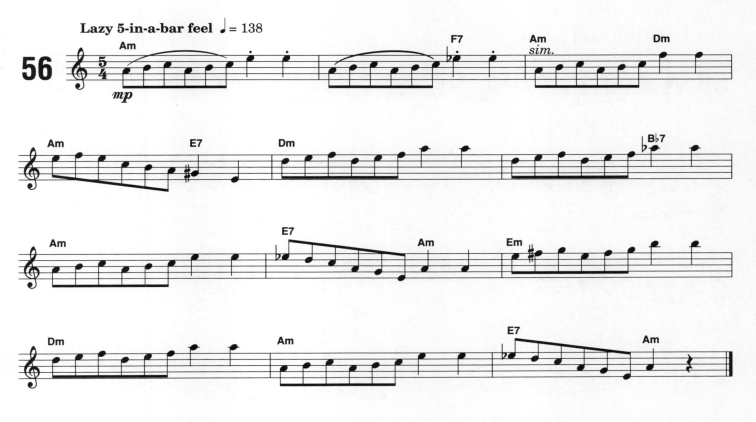

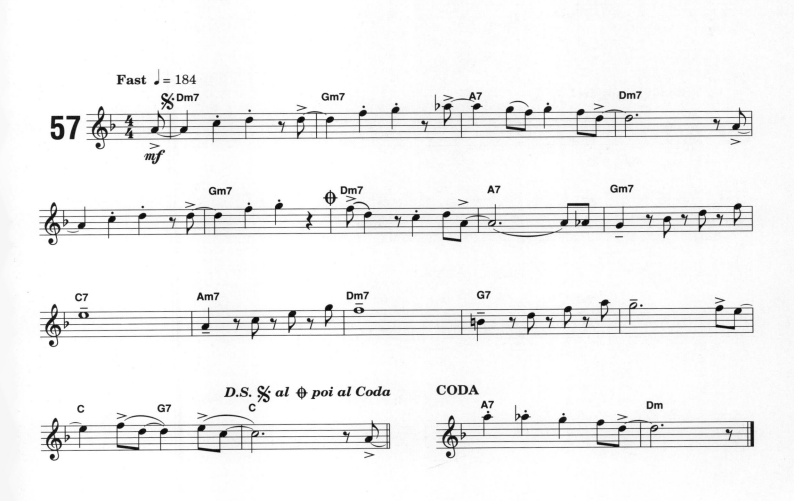

14

3 IMPROVISATION AND BLUES
L'improvisation et le Blues
Improvisation und Blues

Improvisation is the art of spontaneous composition. In jazz it can either be totally free with no restrictions, or over a given chord sequence. The key element in good melodic improvisation is a strong sense of rhythm. By carefully studying Parts 1 and 2 of this book you will by now have developed a good 'feel' for jazz rhythm. This, combined with a firm knowledge of **chords**, will equip you to tackle your first jazz solos.

Chords

A **chord** is simply two or more notes played together. Common **chords** or **triads** are made up of the **first**, **third** and **fifth** notes of the scale. When played separately, the notes of a chord form an **arpeggio**.

eg. C major scale   C major chord

Chords are indicated by **chord symbols**, letter names placed above or below the stave denoting the chord required.

Chord symbols serve two basic purposes:

a) To tell the accompanist what harmony to play.
b) To provide the soloist with a harmonic structure on which he or she can improvise.

Some basic chord symbols explained:

The MAJOR chord

The MINOR chord
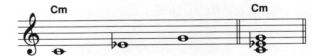

The MAJOR chord plus the *flattened seventh*
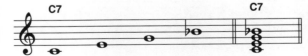

The MAJOR chord plus the *major sixth*

The MAJOR chord plus the *major seventh*

The MINOR chord plus the *flattened seventh*

The DIMINISHED chord (i.e. a chord made up of rising minor thirds)

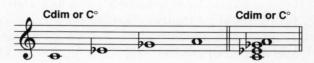

The AUGMENTED chord – the major chord but with a *sharpened fifth* (or a chord made up of major thirds)

The Blues

The **Blues** is probably the most commonly used 'vehicle' in jazz. It usually takes the form of a 12-bar harmonic pattern and works equally well in a swing (♪♪ = ♩³♪) or **rock** context.

In its simplest form a **twelve bar blues** follows this pattern:

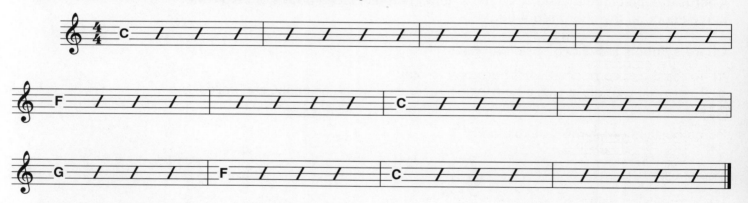

Blues melodies can also be quite simple to allow maximum scope for improvisation. A short phrase repeated three times can work quite successfully:

Basic blues

Try playing this blues round and round, improvising on the notes of the given chords.

The blues scale

As well as chords, another basis for improvisation is the **blues scale**. In its complete form it looks like this:

It is made up of the tonic (1st), sub-dominant (4th) and dominant (5th) plus three **blue notes** — the flattened 3rd, 5th and 7th of the major scale.

Where a **chord symbol** is shown, the player can improvise on the notes of the **blues scale** relating to that chord.

Try playing the *Basic blues* tune and in the rests, improvise your own solos based on the notes of the blues scale. When you have done this try and improvise a solo over the complete tune. It is a good idea to play along with another player so one can play the tune while the other improvises. This will ensure continuity in your music. Now try varying the speed. The Blues works well in both slow and fast tempos.

Remember – in order to play a good jazz solo, a strong sense of rhythm is essential. Make sure that you have worked thoroughly on parts 1 and 2 of this book in order to develop your 'feel' for jazz phrasing.

Riffs

A **riff** is a repeated phrase over which a jazz solo can be improvised.

Latin feel (straight quavers)

65

Try improvising using the notes given above over the **riff**. When you have got the feel of it, try it in different keys.

Here are two more **riffs** over which you can improvise. This time they are in **swing** time (i.e. ♩♩ = ♩ ♪).

Bright swing tempo

66

And finally a sequence using a **jazz rock riff**:

3 Improvisation and Blues
L'IMPROVISATION ET LE BLUES
Improvisation und Blues

L'improvisation est l'art de la composition spontanée. Dans le jazz, elle peut être complètement libre, sans aucune restriction, ou partir d'une succession d'accords déterminés. L'élément primordial d'une bonne improvisation mélodique est le rythme. Maintenant que vous avez étudié la première et la seconde partie de ce livre, vous avez acquis un bon sens du rythme de jazz. Cela vous permettra, avec une solide connaissance des **accords**, de vous attaquer à vos premiers solos de jazz.

Les accords

Un **accord** est simplement formé de deux notes ou plus jouées simultanément. Les **accords** les plus simples, ou **accords parfaits** sont composés de la **tonique**, la **tierce** et la **quinte** de la gamme. Quand on joue ces notes l'une après l'autre, on obtient un **arpège**.

eg. Gamme de do majeur   Accord de do majeur

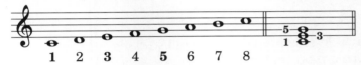

Les accords sont représentés par des **chiffrages**, c'est-à-dire des symboles écrits au dessus ou au dessous de la portée pour désigner l'accord requis.

Les **chiffrages d'accords** remplissent deux rôles:

a) ils indiquent à l'accompagnateur quelle harmonie il doit jouer;
b) ils offrent au soliste une structure harmonique à partir de laquelle il peut improviser.

Voici l'explication de quelques chiffrages d'accords fondamentaux:

l'accord MAJEUR

l'accord MINEUR

l'accord MAJEUR avec *septième mineure*

l'accord MAJEUR avec *sixte ajoutée*

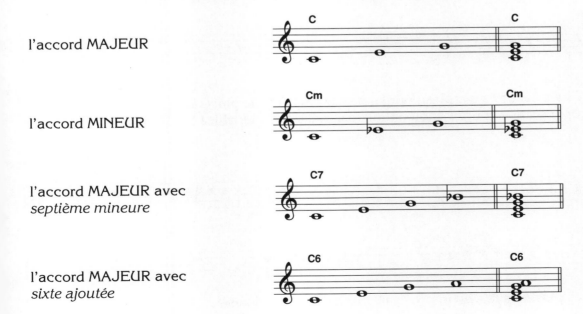

l'accord **MAJEUR** avec
septième majeure

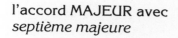

l'accord **MINEUR** avec
septième mineure

l'accord **DIMINUÉ** (c'est à dire,
un accord constitué de tierces
mineures)

l'accord **AUGMENTÉ** – l'accord
majeur avec *quinte augmentée*
(ou un accord constitué de tierces
majeures)

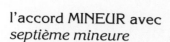

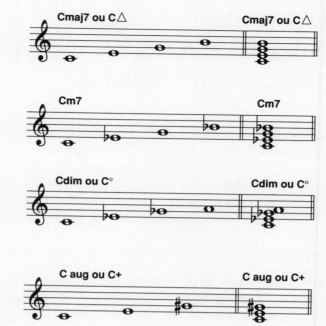

Le Blues

Le **Blues** est probablement le mode d'expression le plus fréquemment utilisé dans
le jazz. Normalement, il se présente sous la forme d'un schéma harmonique de 12
mesures qui s'utilise aussi bien dans le **swing** (♪♪ = ♩ ♪) que dans le **rock**.

Sous sa forme la plus simple, le **Blues de 12 mesures** suit le modèle suivant:

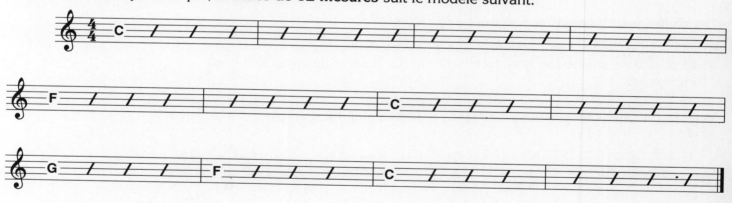

Certaines mélodies de Blues sont très simples pour laisser la plus grande place à
l'improvisation. Une simple phrase courte répétée trois fois, peut être très efficace:

Basic blues (Blues de base)

Essayez de jouer ce blues plusieurs fois en improvisant sur les accords donnés.

La gamme du blues

Avec les accords, **la gamme du blues** est une autre source d'improvisation. La voici sous sa forme complète:

Elle se compose de la tonique (1er degré de la gamme), de la sous-dominante (4ème), de la dominante (5ème), et de trois **notes bleues** – la tierce, la quinte et la septième de la gamme majeure bémolisées.

Lorsque le musicien rencontre un **chiffrage d'accord**, il peut improviser sur les notes de la **gamme du blues** qui correspondent à cet accord.

Essayez de jouer l'air du *Basic blues*, et pendant les pauses improvisez votre propre solo à partir des notes de la gamme du blues. Ensuite, essayez d'improviser un solo sur l'air entier. Il est conseillé de jouer avec quelqu'un d'autre; un musicien joue la mélodie tandis que l'autre improvise, ce qui assure une continuité à votre musique. Après cela, essayez de changer le tempo. Le Blues se joue aussi bien dans un tempo lent que rapide.

Souvenez-vous – pour jouer un bon solo de jazz, le sens du rythme est essentiel. Il faut travailler la première et la seconde partie de ce livre à fond pour développer votre sensibilité au phrasé du jazz.

Le riff

Un **riff** est une phrase répétée sur laquelle on peut improviser un solo de jazz.

Essayez d'improviser sur le **riff** à partir des notes indiquées. Quand vous maîtriserez bien cet exercice, de le jouer dans des tonalités différentes.

Voici deux autres **riffs** pour servir de base à des improvisations. Cette fois-ci, ils sont dans le rythme du **swing** (c'est à dire ♩♩ = ♩ ♪).

Enfin, voici un passage qui utilise un **riff de jazz-rock**:

3 Improvisation and Blues
L'improvisation et le Blues
IMPROVISATION UND BLUES

Improvisation ist die Kunst spontanen Komponierens. Im Jazz wird entweder völlig frei, oder über eine vorgegebene Akkordfolge improvisiert. Ausgeprägtes Rhythmusgefühl ist die Voraussetzung für eine gute melodische Improvisation. Wurden die ersten beiden Teile des Buches sorgfältig durchgearbeitet, wird man nun ein 'Feeling' für Jazzrhythmen entwickelt haben. Ist dazu noch ein solides **Akkordrepertoire** vorhanden, steht dem ersten Jazzsolo nichts mehr im Wege.

Akkorde

Ein **Akkord** besteht aus mindestens zwei Tönen, die gleichzeitig gespielt werden. Normale **Akkorde**, d.h. **Dreiklänge**, setzen sich aus dem **ersten**, **dritten** und **fünften** Ton einer Tonleiter zusammen. Werden die Akkordtöne nacheinander gespielt, so bezeichnet man das als ein **Arpeggio**.

Zum Beispiel C-Dur Tonleiter   C-Dur Akkord

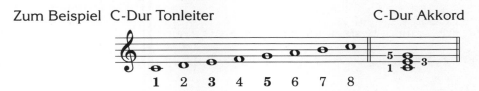

Akkorde werden mit **Akkordsymbolen** gekennzeichnet: Buchstaben über oder unter den Notenlinien benennen den Akkord, der gespielt werden soll.

Akkordsymbole dienen zwei grundsätzlichen Funktionen:

a) Sie zeigen dem Begleiter, welche Harmonie er zu spielen hat.
b) Sie stellen dem Solisten oder der Solistin ein harmonisches Muster bereit, auf das sich seine oder ihre Improvisation stützt.

Erklärung einiger Akkordsymbole:

Der DUR-Dreiklang

Der MOLL-Dreiklang

DUR mit *kleiner Septime*

DUR mit *großer Sexte*

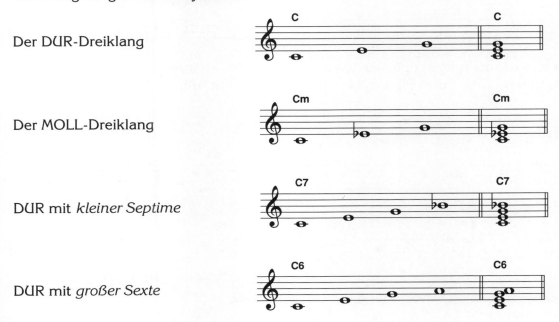

DUR mit *großer Septime*

MOLL mit *kleiner Septime*

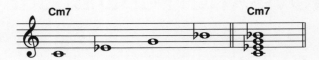

Der **VERMINDERTE** Dreiklang (ein Dreiklang aus übereinandergeschichteten kleinen Terzen)

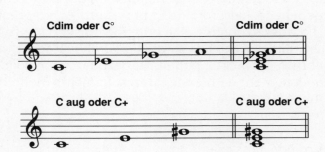

Der **ÜBERMÄSSIGE** Dreiklang – ein Dur-Dreiklang mit *hochalterierter Quinte* (bzw. ein Dreiklang aus übereinandergeschichteten großen Terzen)

Der Blues

Der **Blues**, die wahrscheinlich häufigste Jazzgattung, besteht normalerweise aus einer zwölftaktigen harmonischen Folge, die als **Swing** (♫ = ♩ ♪) und auch als **Rock** gespielt werden kann.

Der einfachsten Version eines **zwölftaktigen Blues** liegt folgendes Munster zugrunde:

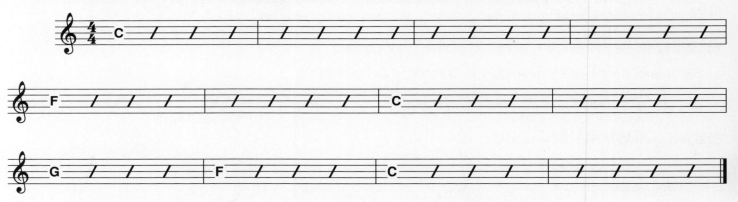

Um der Improvisation optimale Entfaltungsmöglichkeiten zu ermöglichen, können Bluesmelodien recht einfach sein. Eine kurze Phrase, die dreimal wiederholt wird, leistet gute Dienste:

Basic blues (Bluesmodells)

Dieser Blues ist immer wieder zu spielen, während man über die Töne der vorgegebenen Akkorde improvisiert.

Die Bluestonleiter

Neben den Akkorden kann auch die **Bluestonleiter** als Improvisationsgrundlage dienen. Die vollstänige Version dieser Tonleiter sieht folgendermaßen aus:

Sie besteht aus Tonika (erste Stufe), Subdominante (vierte Stufe), Dominante (fünfte Stufe) und aus drei sogenannten **Blue Notes**, nämlich den tiefalterierten Stufen Terz, Quinte und Septime der Durtonleiter.

Dort, wo ein **Akkordsymbol** notiert ist, kann der Spieler mit den Tönen der entsprechenden **Bluestonleiter** improvisieren.

Nun spielt man die Melodie des *Basic blues* und improvisiert in den Pausen eigene Soli mit den Tönen der Bluestonleiter. Danach versucht man, ein Solo über die ganze Melodie zu improvisieren. Es ist empfehlenswert, mit einem zweiten Musiker zusammen zu spielen, indem einer die Melodie spielt und ein anderer improvisiert. Dadurch bleibt die Kontinuität der Musik gewahrt. Jetzt kann man versuchen, in der Geschwindigkeit zu variieren. Für den Blues eignen sich sowohl langsame als auch schnelle Tempi.

Nochmals: Um ein gutes Jazzsolo spielen zu können, braucht man solides Rhythmusgefühl. Die Teile 1 und 2 des Buches müssen sorgfältig durchgearbeitet werden, um ein 'Jazz Feeling' zu entwickeln.

Riffs

Ein **Riff** ist eine wiederholte Phrase, über der ein Jazzsolo improvisiert wird

Mit den oben vorgegebenen Tönen ist über dem **Riff** zu improvisieren. Hat man ein Gefühl dafür entwickelt, versucht man es in anderen Tonarten.

Hier sind zwei weitere **Riffs** über die improvisiert werden kann, diesmal im

Swingrhythmus (d.h. ♪♪ = ♩ ♪).

Und schließlich eine Sequenz über einen **Jazzrock-Riff**: